PRESERVES

Lakeland and Bauer Media Ltd hereby exclude all liability to the extent permitted by law for any errors or omission in this book and for any loss, damage or expense (whether direct or indirect) suffered by a third party relying on any information contained in this book.

This book was created in 2012 for Lakeland by AWW Books, an imprint of Octopus Publishing Group Ltd, based on materials licensed to it by Bauer Media Books, Sydney.

54 Park St, Sydney
GPO Box 4088, Sydney, NSW 2001
phone (02) 9282 8618; fax (02) 9267 9438
www.awwcookbooks.com.au

MEDIA GROUP

OCTOPUS PUBLISHING GROUP
Design – Chris Bell
Food Director – Pamela Clark

Published for Lakeland in the United Kingdom by Octopus Publishing Group Limited

Endeavour House
189 Shaftesbury Avenue
London WC2H 8JY
United Kingdom
phone + 44 (0) 207 632 5400;
fax + 44 (0) 207 632 5405
aww@octopusbooks.co.uk;
www.octopusbooks.co.uk
www.australian-womens-weekly.com

Printed and bound in China

A catalogue record for this book is available from the British Library.

ISBN 978-1-907428-71-5

© Bauer Media Limited 2012
ABN 18 053 273 546

The Department of Health advises that eggs should not be consumed raw. This book contains some dishes made with raw or lightly cooked eggs. It is prudent for vulnerable people such as pregnant and nursing mothers, invalids, the elderly, babies and young children to avoid uncooked or lightly cooked dishes made with eggs. Once prepared, these dishes should be kept refrigerated and used promptly.

This book also includes dishes made with nuts and nut derivatives. It is advisable for those with known allergic reactions to nuts and nut derivatives and those who may be potentially vulnerable to these allergies, such as pregnant and nursing mothers, invalids, the elderly, babies and children to avoid dishes made with nuts and nut oils. It is also prudent to check the labels of pre-prepared ingredients for the possible inclusion of nut derivatives.

Some of the recipes in this book have appeared in other publications.

PRESERVES

There is something very satisfying about making your own homemade preserves. Whether it's an old favourite such as Rhubarb & Orange Marmalade or Green Tomato Chutney or something new – why not try Preserved Lemons or Cracked Olives? – you'll be spoilt for choice with this collection of over 50 sweet and savoury recipes.

One of an exciting new series of cookbooks from Lakeland, *Preserves* is packed with delicious colour photos and expert hints, tips and techniques for beginners and experienced cooks alike.

With every recipe triple-tested® for perfect results, these excellent cookbooks are sure to be some of the best-loved on your kitchen bookshelf. To discover the rest of the range, together with our unrivalled selection of creative kitchenware, visit one of our friendly Lakeland stores or shop online at www.lakeland.co.uk.

CONTENTS

TIPS & TECHNIQUES

Making preserves is very satisfying and is generally straightforward. Here's what you need to know to achieve success every time.

EQUIPMENT

Probably the most important thing is the right pan. Choose a pan made from heavy aluminium, enamel or stainless steel; don't use copper or unsealed cast-iron pans, as the natural acids in fruit and vegetables will damage the surfaces of these pans, spoiling the flavour of the preserve. Don't leave preserve mixtures standing in aluminium pans for more than an hour; once again, natural acids could affect the surface of the pan and the flavour of the preserve.

For successful evaporation, a large, wide-topped pan is essential. A large saucepan is usually fine for most recipes. As a guide to the size of saucepan to use, the preserve mixture should not be more than 5cm deep after all the ingredients have been added to the pan. The saucepan should also have a tight-fitting lid.

A sugar thermometer takes the guess work out of jam making, but it's not essential. A digital thermometer is easy to use and read.

You will also need a large, clean wooden spoon for stirring and a sharp knife for chopping fruit and vegetables.

SUGAR

Unless otherwise specified, use regular granulated white sugar in the recipes in this book. Jams, conserves, marmalades and jellies will benefit by using this coarser sugar; they will be clearer and more sparkling.

Make sure the sugar is dissolved at the stage the recipe indicates. Brush the grains that stick to the side of the pan and wooden spoon back into the mixture using a pastry brush dipped in cold water. Or, put the lid on the pan to cover the hot mixture for a minute or so – this will cause condensation to be trapped under the lid and the drops of moisture formed will wash the sugar grains from the side of the pan back into the preserve mixture.

Warming sugar before it is added to the pan will dissolve the sugar faster, and should result in a clearer jam or jelly. To do this, spread the sugar in a large baking dish, to a maximum depth of 2.5cm. Warm it in a preheated oven at 150°C/130°C fan-assisted. Stir the sugar a few times to warm it through evenly.

Brown sugar, which comes in various shades and flavours from brown through to black, is mostly used in pickles, chutneys, sauces and relishes. The darker the sugar, the richer the flavour.

VINEGAR

Use good-quality vinegar that contains at least 4% acetic acid. Poor-quality vinegars contain less acetic acid and so are not good for preserving.

PECTIN

Pectin is a natural, water-soluble substance found in a variety of fruit and vegetables. When pectin is combined with sugar and acid it develops thickening properties similar to gelatine – this is most obvious in jellies and marmalades and some jams and conserves.

The most common complaint made when making preserves is 'it didn't set'. This can be caused by a lack of pectin in the fruit or an imbalance of pectin and acid – the pectin content of fruit is at its peak when the fruit is slightly under-ripe, that is, before the natural sugars have fully developed.

The fruits that are the best for jam-making are those with a good balance of acid and pectin; they are usually tart or sour in taste and include apples, crab apples, fresh currants, quinces, grapefruit, limes, lemons, sour oranges and plums.

Fruits high in pectin, but low in acid are sweet apples and quinces. It can be the type of fruit that's sweet, or fruit that's become sweet during the ripening process. To counteract this sweetness, and to increase the amount of acid, add 2 tablespoons of fresh lemon juice to each 1kg of fruit used. Or, include some fruit that is low in pectin and high in acid.

Fruits low in pectin, but high in acid are pineapples, apricots, under-ripe peaches and rhubarb. To increase the pectin content, add 2 tablespoons of fresh lemon juice to each 1kg of fruit used. Or, include some fruit that is high in pectin and low in acid.

Fruits low in acid and pectin are berries, melons, pears and cherries. They are not suitable to use alone in jams, and will need the addition of other fruit that contain a proper balance of acid and pectin.

JARS

The jars must be glass and have no chips or cracks; the lids need to be tight-fitting. Usually the lids are made from metal – some poor quality metal lids can corrode if they touch the surface of the preserve during storage. If in doubt, place a disc of baking parchment inside the lid before securing. Metal lids with a lining to prevent contact with the preserve are the best to use. Screw-top lids form a good seal on jars, clip-on plastic lids don't seal as well. Jars that have a clamped-down lid with a rubber seal also work well – it's important that the seal is tight-fitting and firm as old seals lose their grip and can perish in time. If in doubt, buy new seals for the lids.

STERILISING JARS

It's important the jars be as clean as possible; make sure your hands, the preparation area, tea towels and cloths etc., are clean, too. The aim is to finish sterilising the jars and lids at the same time the preserve is ready to be bottled; the hot preserve should be bottled into hot, dry, clean jars. Jars that aren't sterilised properly can cause deterioration of the preserves during storage.

Here are three methods for sterilising jars. Always start with cleaned washed jars and lids.

1 Put the jars and lids through the hottest cycle of a dishwasher without using any detergent.

2 Lie the jars down in a large saucepan with the lids, cover them with cold water then cover the saucepan with a lid. Bring the water to the boil over a high heat and boil the jars for 20 minutes.

3 Stand the jars upright, without touching each other, on a wooden board on the lowest shelf of the oven. Turn the oven to the lowest possible temperature, close the oven door and leave the jars to heat through for 30 minutes.

Next, remove the jars from the oven or dishwasher with a towel, or from the boiling water with tongs and rubber-gloved hands; the water will evaporate from hot wet jars quite quickly. Stand the jars upright and not touching each other on a wooden board, or a bench covered with a towel to protect and insulate the bench.

Pour hot (in most cases) preserves into hot jars until filled to the top (in most cases, unless indicated otherwise by the recipe). Secure the lids tightly, hold the jars firmly with a towel or an oven glove while doing this, then leave the preserves at room temperature to cool before storing.

STORAGE

Most of the recipes say 'store in a cool dark place'. The area needs to have a constant air flow and be dry, cool and dark. Exposure to light during storage will make the preserve discolour. Dank, musty or mouldy conditions will cause preserves to deteriorate. If mould develops on any preserve, throw it away; it is not safe to eat any food that has become mouldy during storage. Once a jar of any preserve is opened, store it in the fridge.

We have given conservatively short keeping times for the recipes in this book, as it's impossible to create a completely sterile environment in a normal home. It's worth knowing that even if the preserve keeps for a year or more, it will gradually change in colour and texture as it ages – usually becoming darker and thicker. It is still fine to eat, providing it smells good and is mould-free.

JELLING POINT

The jelling point is probably the trickiest part of jam-making to get right but you will learn to recognise when jelling point is reached.

The most reliable way to test is by using a sugar thermometer; the temperature – usually 105°C/220°F – will be marked.

Another easy way to tell if jam will jell when it is cold is to remove the jam from the heat and let the bubbles subside. Dip a wooden spoon into the jam and hold the spoon so the bowl faces you. If the jam is ready two or three large drops of jam will roll along the edge of the spoons to form almost a triangle of thick jam.

If you are still in doubt, drop a teaspoon of jam onto a saucer that has been chilled in the fridge or freezer for a few minutes then return the saucer to the freezer until the jam is at room temperature, but not frozen.

• Jam that has pieces of fruit in it should have formed a skin that wrinkles when pushed gently with your finger.

• Jam that has a pulpy texture should be of a spreadable consistency.

• Jelly should be a firm mass on the saucer.

If the jam is not ready, return it to the heat and boil it again until it jells when tested. This may take only a few minutes. If jam refuses to set, try adding about 2 tablespoons of lemon juice or the same amount of sherry, whisky or brandy. Reboil the jam and test again. If all fails, try using

JELLING

1 Dip a wooden spoon into the jam, and hold the bowl of the spoon towards you. If the jam is ready, two or three large drops will roll along the edge of the spoon to form almost a triangle of thick jam.

2 Drop a teaspoon of jam onto a chilled (in the fridge or freezer) saucer. The jam should cool quickly to room temperature.

3 Push the jam with your finger, the skin will wrinkle if the jam is ready. If the jam is not jelling, return it to the heat and boil it again.

MARMALADE

1 Using a large metal spoon, remove and discard any scum from the surface of the marmalade.

2 Use a medium heatproof jug to pour the hot marmalade into hot sterilised jars; seal while hot. Label and date when cold, and store in a cool, dark place.

commercial pectin (available from supermarkets), following the instructions on the packet.

Providing the pectin and acid levels are good, jam will jell when about half the liquid has evaporated. Stir the jam occasionally and gently towards the end of cooking time; do this by dragging the spoon slowly across the base of the pan, just to make sure the jam is not sticking or burning.

HOW TO MAKE PERFECT MARMALADE

1 Choose perfect, slightly under-ripe fruit; wash and dry the fruit.
2 Halve and quarter the fruit; reserve any juice, any trimmings and all the seeds. Cut through the quarters to make the rind as thick or as thin as you like.
3 Combine any trimmings with

the seeds in a muslin bag. Put the fruit, juice and muslin bag in a large non-metallic bowl. Add enough cold water to the bowl to barely cover the fruit and to make it just barely float. Cover the bowl, and stand it overnight.
4 Put the undrained fruit mixture into a small saucepan, cover and bring the mixture to the boil over high heat. Reduce the heat and simmer between 30 minutes to 1 hour, depending on the fruit, until the rind is tender and mushy.
5 Measure the fruit mixture using a heatproof jug, allow 1 cup of white granulated sugar to each cup of fruit mixture. Return the fruit mixture and the sugar to the saucepan – this mixture should not be more than 5cm deep.
6 Stir the mixture over a high heat, without boiling, until the sugar is dissolved. Boil the mixture

rapidly until the marmalade will jell when tested on a cold saucer.
7 Stand the marmalade 10 minutes; remove and discard any scum from the surface of the marmalade, using a large metal spoon. Next, use a medium heatproof jug to pour the hot jam into hot sterilised jars, seal while hot. Label and date the jars when cold and store them in a cool, dark place.

JELLIES

A properly made jelly should be sparkling clear and have a slight wobble, but still be firm enough to hold its shape when 'cut' with a teaspoon. Similar rules about pectin, acid, ripeness, boiling, storing, etc, apply to jellies as well as jams.

Here is a basic method to use for fruits such as sour apples, crab apples, quinces and grapes:
1 Wash the fruit well, cutting away any damaged parts. Chop the fruit very roughly and put it into a saucepan with seeds, skins, stems, etc. This mixture should not be any deeper than 2.5 cm.

JELLIES

Secure a clean, damp cloth to the legs of an upturned stool, or use a jelly straining kit, as pictured. The cloth should sag, so that the heavy fruit mixture drips into a bowl below.

2 Add enough water to barely cover the fruit – the fruit should just begin to float. The mixture should be about 5cm deep at this stage.

3 Cover the saucepan with a tight-fitting lid, bring to the boil over a high heat, then reduce the heat until the mixture simmers gently. Cook, covered, until the fruit is pulpy – this could take an hour or more, depending on the type of fruit and its degree of ripeness.

4 While the fruit is cooking, prepare a cloth to strain the fruit mixture through. Use a fine cloth, such as a thoroughly soaked (if new) then washed and rinsed muslin, sheeting or unbleached calico. Jelly straining kits can be bought from specialty kitchenware shops, or make a jelly bag by securing the dampened cloth to the legs of an upturned stool. The cloth should sag, so that the heavy fruit mixture drips into a bowl below.

5 Pour the fruit mixture into the cloth, cover loosely with plastic to keep it clean; leave the fruit mixture to drip into the bowl for 12 hours or so. Don't squeeze or push the fruit through the cloth, as this will cause the jelly to be cloudy.

6 Do a quick pectin test to judge how much sugar is needed for this basic recipe. Put a teaspoon of the fruit liquid into a cup or glass, and add 3 teaspoons methylated spirits. Stir the mixture gently, if it forms a fairly solid, jelly-like clot, the fruit liquid is high in pectin, in which case allow 1 cup fruit liquid to 1 cup of sugar. This means the jelly will jell quickly so, be aware that the cooking time could be as little as 10 minutes. Use a sugar thermometer or the saucer test to establish if the jelly has jelled. If several smaller clots appear after stirring the methylated spirits and fruit liquid together, use ¾ cup sugar to each 1 cup of fruit liquid. If the mixture doesn't clot, or if the clots are tiny, use the lesser amount of sugar and add 2 tablespoons lemon juice to the mixture after the sugar has been dissolved. If all else fails, resort to using a commercial pectin to set the jelly, following the packet directions. We have coloured the fruit liquid – which is usually fairly clear – to make it easier for you to see the pectin test (below).

7 Return the fruit liquid to the saucepan; it should be no more than 2.5cm deep. Bring the liquid to the boil, uncovered. Add the sugar, stir over a high heat, without boiling, until the sugar is dissolved. Boil rapidly, uncovered – it will be foamy – without stirring, until the mixture jells when tested. Remove the jelly from the heat, allow the bubbles to subside and skim and discard any scum from the surface of the jelly.

8 Use a medium heatproof jug to pour the hot jelly into the hot sterilised jars. Seal the jars while hot. Label and date when cold, and store in a cool dark place.

PECTIN TEST

A pectin test will tell how much sugar is needed (see method left). Stir the mixture gently, if it forms a fairly solid jelly-like clot, the fruit liquid is high in pectin.

JAMS & JELLIES

BLUEBERRY & APPLE JAM

1kg blueberries
3 medium green-skinned apples
   (450g), peeled, cored, chopped
   finely
2 tablespoons lemon juice
880g granulated sugar

1 Combine berries, apples and juice in large saucepan; bring to the boil. Reduce heat; simmer, uncovered, about 15 minutes or until berries are soft.
2 Add sugar to pan; stir over high heat, without boiling, until sugar dissolves. Bring to the boil; boil, uncovered, without stirring, about 20 minutes or until jam jells when tested.
3 Pour hot jam into hot sterilised jars; seal immediately. Label and date jars when cold.

prep + cook time 35 minutes
makes 1.25 litres
nutritional count per tablespoon
0g total fat (0g saturated fat); 284kJ (68 cal); 17.2g carbohydrate; 0.1g protein; 0.4g fibre
tip Granny Smith apples are best for this recipe.

APRICOT & VANILLA JAM

1kg fresh apricots, halved, stones
  removed
1 vanilla pod, halved lengthways
250ml water
1kg granulated sugar

1 Combine apricots, vanilla pod and the water in large saucepan; bring to the boil. Reduce heat; simmer, covered, about 15 minutes or until mixture is pulpy.

2 Add sugar to pan; stir over high heat, without boiling, until sugar dissolves. Bring to the boil; boil, uncovered, without stirring, about 35 minutes or until jam jells when tested.

3 Discard vanilla pod. Pour hot jam into hot sterilised jars; seal immediately. Label and date jars when cold.

prep + cook time 55 minutes
makes 1 litre
nutritional count per tablespoon
0g total fat (0g saturated fat); 694kJ (166 cal); 43g carbohydrate; 0.1g protein; 0.4g fibre

SPICED PLUM & PORT JAM

1kg plums, stones removed,
quartered
60ml orange juice
250ml water
1 cinnamon stick, halved
½ teaspoon cloves
1 star anise
1.1kg granulated sugar,
approximately
125ml port

1 Combine plums, juice and the water in large saucepan; bring to the boil. Reduce heat; simmer, uncovered, about 15 minutes or until plums are pulpy.

2 Meanwhile, tie cinnamon, cloves and star anise in muslin.

3 Measure fruit mixture, allow 1 cup sugar to each cup of fruit mixture. Return fruit mixture, sugar, port and muslin bag to pan; stir over high heat, without boiling, until sugar dissolves. Bring to the boil; boil, uncovered, without stirring, about 35 minutes or until jam jells when tested.

4 Discard muslin bag. Pour hot jam into hot sterilised jars; seal immediately. Label and date jars when cold.

prep + cook time 55 minutes
makes 1 litre
nutritional count per tablespoon
0g total fat (0g saturated fat);
414kJ (99 cal); 24.6g carbohydrate;
0.1g protein; 0.4g fibre

STRAWBERRY & ORANGE CONSERVE

1.5 kg strawberries, hulled
1.1kg granulated sugar
125ml orange juice
2 tablespoons lemon juice
1 tablespoon finely grated orange rind
1 tablespoon orange-flavoured liqueur

1 Cook berries in large saucepan, covered, over low heat, about 5 minutes to extract some juice from the berries. Remove berries from pan with slotted spoon; set aside in medium bowl.

2 Add sugar and juices to berry juice in pan; stir over high heat, without boiling, until sugar dissolves. Bring to the boil; boil, uncovered, without stirring, about 30 minutes.

3 Return berries to pan, reduce heat; simmer, uncovered, about 20 minutes or until jam jells when tested. Remove from heat; stir in rind and liqueur.

4 Pour hot jam into hot sterilised jars; seal immediately. Label and date jars when cold.

prep + cook time 1 hour 15 minutes
makes 1.25 litres
nutritional count per tablespoon 0g total fat (0g saturated fat); 326kJ (78 cal); 19.4g carbohydrate; 0.4g protein; 0.6g fibre

CHERRY JAM

1kg cherries, halved, pitted
2 medium pears (460g), peeled,
    cored, chopped finely
80ml lemon juice
250ml water
880g granulated sugar,
    approximately

1 Combine cherries, pear, juice and the water in large saucepan; bring to the boil. Reduce heat; simmer, covered, about 15 minutes or until cherries are soft.

2 Measure fruit mixture; allow 1 cup sugar for each cup of fruit mixture. Return fruit mixture and sugar to pan; stir over high heat, without boiling, until sugar dissolves. Bring to the boil; boil, uncovered, without stirring, about 30 minutes or until jam jells when tested.

3 Pour hot jam into hot sterilised jars; seal immediately. Label and date jars when cold.

prep + cook time 1 hour
makes 1 litre
nutritional count per tablespoon
0g total fat (0g saturated fat); 347kJ (83 cal); 21.2g carbohydrate; 0.2g protein; 0.4g fibre

RASPBERRY & MINT JAM

6 sprigs fresh mint, chopped
  coarsely
1kg raspberries
2 tablespoons lemon juice
1kg granulated sugar

1 Tie mint in muslin. Combine berries, muslin bag and juice in large saucepan; cook over low heat, stirring occasionally, about 5 minutes or until berries are soft.
2 Add sugar; stir over high heat, without boiling, until sugar dissolves. Bring to the boil; boil, uncovered, without stirring, about 15 minutes or until jam jells when tested.
3 Discard muslin bag. Pour hot jam into hot sterilised jars; seal immediately. Label and date jars when cold.

prep + cook time 30 minutes
makes 1.25 litres
nutritional count per tablespoon
0.1g total fat (0g saturated fat); 301kJ (72 cal); 17.7g carbohydrate; 0.2g protein; 1g fibre

PEACH, RASPBERRY & CHAMPAGNE JAM

500 g peaches, peeled, stones removed, finely chopped
500g raspberries
330g granulated sugar
1 tablespoon lemon juice
125ml pink champagne

1 Combine peaches, berries, sugar, juice and half the champagne in large saucepan; stir over high heat, without boiling, until sugar dissolves. Bring to the boil; boil, uncovered, without stirring, about 15 minutes or until jam jells when tested. Stir in remaining champagne.
2 Pour hot jam into hot sterilised jars; seal immediately. Label and date jars when cold.

prep + cook time 35 minutes
makes 750ml
nutritional count per tablespoon
0.1g total fat (0g saturated fat); 196kJ (47 cal); 11g carbohydrate; 0.3g protein; 1g fibre

MANDARIN & DRIED APRICOT JAM

2 large mandarins (500g)
1 medium lemon (140g)
125g dried apricots, chopped
    coarsely
750ml water
660g granulated sugar,
    approximately

1 Using a vegetable peeler, peel rind thinly from mandarins and lemon, without removing any white pith. Shred rind finely. Discard pith and membranes from mandarins and lemon; chop flesh coarsely, discard seeds.

2 Combine fruit, apricots and the water in large saucepan; bring to the boil. Reduce heat; simmer, covered, about 30 minutes or until rind softens.

3 Measure fruit mixture, allow 1 cup sugar for each cup of fruit mixture. Return fruit mixture and sugar to pan; stir over high heat, without boiling, until sugar dissolves. Bring to the boil; boil, uncovered, without stirring, about 40 minutes or until jam jells when tested.

4 Pour hot jam into hot sterilised jars; seal immediately. Label and date jars when cold.

prep + cook time 1 hour 30 minutes
makes 1 litre
nutritional count per tablespoon 0g total fat (0g saturated fat); 260kJ (62 cal); 15.6g carbohydrate; 0.2g protein; 0.5g fibre

ANY BERRY JAM

125g blackberries
125g blueberries
250g raspberries
500g strawberries, hulled
80ml lemon juice
880g granulated sugar

1 Stir ingredients in large saucepan over high heat, without boiling, until sugar dissolves; bring to the boil. Reduce heat; simmer, uncovered, without stirring, about 30 minutes or until jam jells when tested.
2 Pour hot jam into hot sterilised jars; seal immediately. Label and date jars when cold.

prep + cook time 40 minutes
makes 1 litre
nutritional count per tablespoon 0g total fat (0g saturated fat); 326kJ (78 cal); 19.5g carbohydrate; 0.3g protein; 0.7g fibre
tip Use any combination of berries you like to collectively weigh 1kg.

CHUNKY FIG & VANILLA JAM

1kg fresh whole figs
125ml orange juice
2 tablespoons lemon juice
1 vanilla pod, halved lengthways
660g granulated sugar

1 Cut each unpeeled fig into eight wedges. Combine figs, juices and vanilla pod in large saucepan; bring to the boil. Reduce heat; simmer, covered, about 20 minutes or until figs are soft.

2 Add sugar to pan; stir over high heat, without boiling, until sugar dissolves. Bring to the boil; boil, uncovered, without stirring, about 30 minutes or until jam jells when tested. Discard vanilla pod.

3 Pour hot jam into hot sterilised jars; seal immediately. Label and date jars when cold.

prep + cook time 1 hour
makes 750 ml
nutritional count per tablespoon
0.1g total fat (0g saturated fat); 351kJ (84 cal); 20.9g carbohydrate; 0.4g protein; 0.7g fibre
tips You can use any variety of fresh fig for this recipe. Omit the vanilla pod for a plain fig jam.

REDCURRANT JELLY

1.5kg redcurrants
2 tablespoons lemon juice
1.5 litres water, approximately
1.3kg granulated sugar

1 Combine currants, juice and the water in large saucepan (water should barely cover currants); bring to the boil. Reduce heat; simmer, covered, about 20 minutes.
2 Strain mixture through a fine cloth into large bowl. Stand 3 hours or overnight until liquid stops dripping. Do not squeeze cloth; discard pulp.
3 Return redcurrant liquid to pan; bring to the boil. Add sugar; stir over high heat, without boiling, until sugar dissolves. Bring to the boil; boil rapidly, uncovered, without stirring, about 45 minutes or until jelly jells when tested.
4 Pour hot jelly into hot sterilised jars; seal immediately. Label and date jars when cold.

prep + cook time 1 hour 10 minutes + standing time
makes 1.75 litres
nutritional count per tablespoon
0g total fat (0g saturated fat); 259kJ (62 cal); 16.9g carbohydrate; 0.3g protein; 0.7g fibre

APPLE JELLY

1kg green-skinned apples,
   unpeeled, chopped coarsely
1.5 litres water
1.3kg granulated sugar,
   approximately

1 Combine apple, including core and seeds, and the water in large saucepan; bring to the boil. Reduce heat; simmer, covered, about 1 hour or until pulpy.
2 Strain mixture through a fine cloth into large bowl. Stand 3 hours or overnight until liquid stops dripping. Do not squeeze cloth; discard pulp.
3 Measure apple liquid, allow 1 cup sugar for each cup of liquid. Return apple liquid and sugar to pan; stir over high heat, without boiling, until sugar dissolves. Bring to the boil; boil rapidly, uncovered, without stirring, about 20 minutes or until jelly jells when tested.
4 Pour hot jelly into hot sterilised jars; seal immediately. Label and date jars when cold.

prep + cook time 1 hour 45 minutes + standing time
makes 1.25 litres
nutritional count per tablespoon
0g total fat (0g saturated fat); 372kJ (89 cal); 23.1g carbohydrate; 0g protein; 0.3g fibre
tips Granny Smith apples are best for this recipe. This is a good base jelly – for slight variations try adding cinnamon sticks, rosemary sprigs or dried lavender to the jelly.

MINT JELLY

1kg green-skinned apples,
  unpeeled, chopped coarsely
1.5 litres water
1.2kg granulated sugar,
  approximately
green food colouring
2 good handfuls fresh mint leaves

1 Combine apple and the water in large saucepan; bring to the boil. Reduce heat; simmer, covered, about 1 hour or until apple is pulpy.
2 Strain mixture through a fine cloth into large bowl. Stand 3 hours or overnight until liquid stops dripping. Do not squeeze cloth; discard pulp.
3 Measure apple liquid; allow 1 cup sugar for each cup of liquid. Return apple liquid and sugar to same pan; stir over high heat, without boiling, until sugar dissolves. Bring to the boil; boil rapidly, uncovered, without stirring, about 30 minutes or until jelly jells when tested.
4 Pour jelly into large heatproof jug; stir in a little food colouring. Stand until jelly is lukewarm (but not set).
5 Meanwhile, drop mint into small saucepan of boiling water for 2 seconds; drain. Rinse under cold water; drain, pat dry with absorbent paper. Chop mint finely; stir into lukewarm jelly.
6 Pour jelly into hot sterilised jars; seal immediately. Label and date jars when cold.

prep + cook time 2 hours + standing time
makes 1.5 litres
nutritional count per tablespoon
0g total fat (0g saturated fat); 288kJ (69 cal); 17.9g carbohydrate; 0.1g protein; 0.2g fibre
tips Granny Smith apples are best for this recipe. Store mint jelly in a cool, dark place for 3 months. Refrigerate after opening. The jelly has a natural soft pink colour before the colouring is used, you might prefer to omit the colouring.

MARMALADES

MASTER ORANGE MARMALADE

1kg oranges
1.5 litres water
1kg granulated sugar,
    approximately

1 Peel oranges, removing rind and white pith separately; slice rind thinly, reserve half the pith. Quarter oranges; slice flesh thinly, reserve any seeds. Tie reserved pith and seeds in muslin.

2 Combine rind, flesh, muslin bag and the water in large saucepan; bring to the boil. Reduce heat; simmer, covered, about 1 hour or until rind is soft. Discard muslin bag.

3 Measure fruit mixture, allow 1 cup sugar for each cup of fruit mixture. Return orange mixture and sugar to pan; stir over high heat, without boiling, until sugar dissolves. Bring to the boil; boil, uncovered, without stirring, about 30 minutes or until marmalade jells when tested.

4 Pour hot marmalade into hot sterilised jars; seal immediately. Label and date jars when cold.

prep + cook time 1 hour 45 minutes
makes 1 litre
nutritional count per tablespoon
0g total fat (0g saturated fat); 368kJ (88 cal); 22.5g carbohydrate; 0.2g protein; 0.4g fibre
tip This basic method of making marmalade will work with most citrus fruits including grapefruit, lemons, tangerines and limes or various combinations of these fruits.

RHUBARB & ORANGE MARMALADE

1kg oranges
1kg trimmed rhubarb, chopped
  coarsely
1.3kg granulated sugar

1 Peel oranges; slice rind with pith thinly. Squeeze juice from oranges (you need 375 ml juice).
2 Combine rind, juice, rhubarb and sugar in large saucepan; stir over high heat, without boiling, until sugar dissolves. Bring to the boil; boil, uncovered, without stirring, about 45 minutes or until marmalade jells when tested.
3 Pour hot marmalade into hot sterilised jars; seal immediately. Label and date jars when cold.

prep + cook time 1 hour 15 minutes
makes 1.5 litres
nutritional count per tablespoon 0g total fat (0g saturated fat); 326kJ (78 cal); 19.4g carbohydrate; 0.3g protein; 0.6g fibre
tip For best results use only the reddest parts of the rhubarb stems.

CRANBERRY & LEMON MARMALADE

7 medium lemons (980g)
1 litre water
300g fresh or frozen cranberries
1.1kg granulated sugar

1 Halve 5 lemons, then slice thinly, reserving any seeds and juice. Juice and seed remaining lemons. Tie seeds in muslin.

2 Combine lemon slices, juice, muslin bag and the water in large saucepan, bring to the boil; boil, uncovered, about 1 hour or until rind is soft, adding cranberries for the last 20 minutes of cooking time. Discard muslin bag.

3 Add sugar to pan; stir over high heat, without boiling, until sugar dissolves. Bring to the boil; boil, uncovered, about 15 minutes or until marmalade jells when tested.

4 Pour hot marmalade into hot sterilised jars; seal immediately. Label and date jars when cold.

prep + cook time 1 hour 30 minutes
makes 1.75 litres
nutritional count per tablespoon
0g total fat (0g saturated fat); 226kJ (54 cal); 13.4g carbohydrate; 0.1g protein; 0.4g fibre

MANDARIN MARMALADE

1kg mandarins
60ml lemon juice
1 litre water
1.1kg granulated sugar,
   approximately

1 Combine whole mandarins, juice and the water in large saucepan; bring to the boil. Reduce heat; simmer, covered, about 45 minutes or until fruit is soft.
2 Remove mandarins from liquid; reserve liquid. Coarsely chop mandarins, including rind; discard seeds. Return chopped mandarin to reserved liquid.
3 Measure fruit mixture, allow 1 cup sugar for each cup of fruit mixture. Return fruit mixture and sugar to pan; stir over high heat, without boiling, until sugar dissolves. Bring to the boil; boil, uncovered, without stirring, about 30 minutes or until jam jells when tested.
4 Pour hot marmalade into hot sterilised jars; seal immediately. Label and date jars when cold.

prep + cook time 1 hour 15 minutes
makes 1 litre
nutritional count per tablespoon
0g total fat (0g saturated fat); 405kJ (97 cal); 24.6g carbohydrate; 0.2g protein; 0.4g fibre

OVERNIGHT THREE-CITRUS PROCESSOR MARMALADE

1 medium grapefruit (425g), chopped coarsely

1 medium lemon (140g), chopped coarsely

2 large oranges (600g), chopped coarsely

1 litre water

1.75kg granulated sugar

1 Process fruit, including rind and seeds, in batches, until chopped finely.

2 Combine fruit and the water in large saucepan; bring to the boil. Reduce heat; simmer, covered, 30 minutes. Remove from heat; stand, covered, overnight.

3 Add sugar to fruit mixture in pan; stir over high heat, without boiling, until sugar dissolves. Bring to the boil; boil, uncovered, without stirring, about 40 minutes or until marmalade jells when tested.

4 Pour hot marmalade into hot sterilised jars; seal immediately. Label and date jars when cold.

prep + cook time 1 hour 15 minutes + standing time
makes 2 litres
nutritional count per tablespoon
0g total fat (0g saturated fat); 309kJ (74 cal); 19g carbohydrate; 0.1g protein; 0.2g fibre

ORANGE, CORIANDER & GINGER MARMALADE

4 large oranges (1.2kg)
1 tablespoon coriander seeds, crushed
5cm piece fresh root ginger (25g), sliced thinly
1 litre water
1.1kg granulated sugar

1 Cut oranges in half. Squeeze juice; reserve juice and seeds separately. Tie reserved seeds, coriander seeds and ginger in muslin bag.
2 Using a sharp knife, remove rind as thinly as possible from orange halves; discard pith. Cut rind into thin strips.
3 Combine rind, reserved juice, muslin bag and the water in large saucepan; bring to the boil. Reduce heat; simmer, covered, about 1 hour or until rind is soft. Discard muslin bag.
4 Add sugar; stir over high heat, without boiling, until sugar dissolves. Bring to the boil; boil, uncovered, without stirring, about 40 minutes or until marmalade jells when tested.
5 Pour hot marmalade into hot sterilised jars; seal immediately. Label and date jars when cold.

prep + cook time 1 hour 45 minutes
makes 1.25 litres
nutritional count per tablespoon
0g total fat (0g saturated fat); 318kJ (76 cal); 19.6g carbohydrate; 0.2g protein; 0.3g fibre
tip You can cut the rind into strips as thin or thick as you like; adjust the cooking time accordingly.

KUMQUAT MARMALADE

1kg kumquats
2 tablespoons lemon juice
1.25 litres water
1.3kg granulated sugar

1 Quarter kumquats, being careful not to cut all the way through. Squeeze kumquats to release seeds. Tie seeds in muslin. Process kumquats until finely chopped. Combine kumquats, muslin bag, juice and the water in large saucepan; stand, covered, overnight.

2 Bring kumquat mixture to the boil. Reduce heat; simmer, covered, about 30 minutes or until rind is soft. Discard muslin bag.

3 Add sugar; stir over high heat, without boiling, until sugar dissolves. Bring to the boil; boil, uncovered, without stirring, about 30 minutes or until marmalade jells when tested.

4 Pour hot marmalade into hot sterilised jars; seal immediately. Label and date jars when cold.

prep + cook time 1 hour 30 minutes + standing time
makes 1.5 litres
nutritional count per tablespoon
0g total fat (0g saturated fat); 314kJ (75 cal); 19.2g carbohydrate; 0.1g protein; 0.3g fibre

THICK-CUT DARK WHISKY MARMALADE

4 large oranges (1.2kg)
2 medium lemons (280g)
1.5 litres water
440g granulated sugar,
     approximately
440g dark brown sugar,
     approximately
2 tablespoons treacle
2 tablespoons whisky

1 Peel oranges and lemons thickly; slice peel thickly, chop flesh coarsely. Discard seeds.

2 Combine peel, flesh and the water in large saucepan; bring to the boil. Reduce heat; simmer, covered, about 1 hour or until rind is soft.

3 Measure fruit mixture, allow ½ cup of each sugar for each cup of fruit mixture. Return fruit mixture, sugar and treacle to pan; stir over high heat, without boiling, until sugar dissolves. Bring to the boil; boil, uncovered, without stirring, about 40 minutes or until marmalade jells when tested. Stir in whisky.

4 Pour hot marmalade into hot sterilised jars; seal immediately. Label and date jars when cold.

prep + cook time 1 hour 45 minutes
makes 1.25 litres
nutritional count per tablespoon 0g total fat (0g saturated fat); 284kJ (68 cal); 16.7g carbohydrate; 0.3g protein; 0.5g fibre

CHUTNEYS, PICKLES & RELISHES

BEETROOT CHUTNEY

6 medium fresh beetroot (1kg), trimmed
2 teaspoons cumin seeds
1 cinnamon stick, broken
4 cardamom pods, bruised
4 large green-skinned apples (800g), peeled, cored, chopped coarsely
1 medium red onion (170g), chopped coarsely
2 cloves garlic, crushed
2cm piece fresh root ginger (10g) grated
220g granulated sugar
500ml white vinegar
2 tablespoons lemon juice
1 teaspoon coarse cooking salt

1 Boil, steam or microwave beetroot until tender; drain. When cool enough to handle, peel beetroot. Finely chop half the beetroot; blend or process remaining beetroot until smooth.
2 Tie spices in muslin. Combine puréed beetroot and muslin bag with apple, onion, garlic, ginger, sugar, vinegar, juice and salt in large saucepan; stir over high heat, without boiling, until sugar dissolves. Bring to the boil. Reduce heat; simmer, uncovered, stirring occasionally, 30 minutes. Add chopped beetroot; simmer, uncovered, about 10 minutes or until chutney is thick. Discard muslin bag.
3 Spoon hot chutney into hot sterilised jars; seal immediately. Label and date jars when cold.

prep + cook time 1 hour 15 minutes
makes 1.5 litres
nutritional count per tablespoon
0g total fat (0g saturated fat); 96kJ (23 cal); 5.1g carbohydrate; 0.3g protein; 0.6g fibre
tips Granny Smith apples are best for this recipe. Store chutney in a cool, dark place for at least three weeks before opening. Wear disposable gloves when peeling beetroot as it does stain hands. Refrigerate after opening.

GREEN TOMATO CHUTNEY

2kg green tomatoes, cored, chopped coarsely
2 large brown onions (400g), chopped coarsely
2 large green-skinned apples (400g), peeled, cored, chopped coarsely
440g unrefined granulated sugar
625ml cider vinegar
150g sultanas
4 fresh long red chillies, chopped finely
6 cloves garlic, chopped finely
2 teaspoons coarse cooking salt

1 Stir ingredients in large saucepan over high heat, without boiling, until sugar dissolves; bring to the boil. Reduce heat; simmer, uncovered, stirring occasionally, about 1½ hours or until chutney is thick.
2 Spoon hot chutney into hot sterilised jars; seal immediately. Label and date jars when cold.

prep + cook time 2 hours
makes 1.25 litres
nutritional count per tablespoon 0.1g total fat (0g saturated fat); 201kJ (48 cal); 10.8g carbohydrate; 0.5g protein; 0.8g fibre
tips Granny Smith apples are best for this recipe. Store chutney in a cool, dark place for at least three weeks before opening. Refrigerate after opening. This recipe is quite spicy; for a milder version you can remove the seeds from the chillies or use less chilli.

MANGO CHUTNEY

3 medium mangoes (1.3kg), chopped coarsely
150g coarsely chopped dried apricots
2 medium red onions (340g), chopped finely
330g light brown sugar
500ml cider vinegar
6 cloves garlic, chopped finely
1 teaspoon ground ginger
½ teaspoon dried chilli flakes
1 teaspoon coarse cooking salt

1 Stir ingredients in large saucepan over high heat, without boiling, until sugar dissolves; bring to the boil. Reduce heat; simmer, uncovered, stirring occasionally, about 1 hour or until chutney is thick.

2 Spoon hot chutney into hot sterilised jars; seal immediately. Label and date jars when cold.

prep + cook time 1 hour 15 minutes
makes 1 litre
nutritional count per tablespoon 0.1g total fat (0g saturated fat); 196kJ (47cal); 10.7g carbohydrate; 0.5g protein; 0.7g fibre
tip Store chutney in a cool, dark place for at least three weeks before opening. Refrigerate after opening.

PEACH & GINGER CHUTNEY

1.8kg peaches (almost ripe), peeled, chopped coarsely
150g raisins
1 large red onion (300g), chopped coarsely
330g granulated sugar
500ml cider vinegar
8cm piece fresh root ginger (40g), grated
2 fresh long red chillies, halved, sliced thinly
1 cinnamon stick
1 teaspoon coarse cooking salt

1 Stir ingredients in large saucepan over high heat, without boiling, until sugar dissolves; bring to the boil. Reduce heat; simmer, uncovered, stirring occasionally, about 1¼ hours or until chutney is thick. Discard cinnamon stick.
2 Spoon hot chutney into hot sterilised jars; seal immediately. Label and date jars when cold.

prep + cook time 2 hours
makes 1.4 litres
nutritional count per tablespoon
0g total fat (0g saturated fat); 150kJ (36 cal); 8.4g carbohydrate; 0.3g protein; 0.5g fibre
tips Depending on the ripeness of the peaches, peel them using a vegetable peeler or, blanch them by cutting a small cross in the base of each peach; cover with boiling water in a heatproof bowl. Stand 5 minutes, then transfer peaches to a bowl of iced water. Using fingers or a small knife, carefully remove the skin. Store chutney in a cool, dark place for at least three weeks before opening. Refrigerate after opening.

CHILLI JAM

1kg ripe plum tomatoes, chopped coarsely
500g caster sugar
80ml white vinegar
60ml lemon juice
6 fresh long red chillies, sliced thinly
2 fresh small red thai chillies, sliced thinly
4cm piece fresh root ginger (20g), grated
3 cloves garlic, crushed
2 tablespoons fish sauce
1 teaspoon coarse cooking salt

1 Stir ingredients in large saucepan over high heat, without boiling, until sugar dissolves. Bring to the boil. Reduce heat; simmer, uncovered, stirring occasionally, about 1¼ hours or until jam is thick. Cool 15 minutes.

2 Blend or process chilli mixture, in batches, until smooth. Pour into hot sterilised jars; seal immediately. Label and date jars when cold.

prep + cook time 1 hour 45 minutes + cooling time
makes about 830ml
nutritional count per tablespoon 0g total fat (0g saturated fat); 226kJ (54 cal); 13.1g carbohydrate; 0.4g protein; 0.4g fibre
tips Store in a cool, dark place for up to three months. Refrigerate after opening. Wear plastic disposable gloves when cutting chillies as they can burn your skin.

SWEET FRUIT CHUTNEY

1kg green-skinned apples, peeled, cored, chopped coarsely

800g tomatoes, peeled, chopped coarsely

2 large brown onions (400g), chopped coarsely

150g coarsely chopped dried apricots

140g coarsely chopped seeded dried dates

160g dried currants

2cm piece fresh root ginger (10g), grated

625ml malt vinegar

440g light brown sugar

2 teaspoons mixed spice

¼ teaspoon cayenne pepper

1 tablespoon coarse cooking salt

1 Stir ingredients in large saucepan over high heat, without boiling, until sugar dissolves; bring to the boil. Reduce heat; simmer, uncovered, stirring occasionally, about 1½ hours or until chutney is thick.

2 Spoon hot chutney into hot sterilised jars; seal immediately. Label and date jars when cold.

prep + cook time 2 hours
makes 2.25 litres
nutritional count per tablespoon
0g total fat (0g saturated fat); 138kJ (33 cal); 7.5g carbohydrate; 0.3g protein; 0.6g fibre
tips Granny Smith apples are best for this recipe. Store chutney in a cool, dark place for at least three weeks before opening. Refrigerate after opening.

PLOUGHMAN'S PICKLE

215g coarse cooking salt
500ml boiling water
1.75 litres cold water
2 large brown onions (400g), chopped finely
1 small cauliflower (1kg), cut into small florets
5 large courgettes (750g), chopped finely
2 stalks celery (300g), trimmed, chopped finely
2 large green-skinned apples (400g), peeled, cored, chopped coarsely
3 cloves garlic, crushed
1 litre malt vinegar
50g cornflour
660g light brown sugar
3 teaspoons ground turmeric
2 teaspoons each ground cinnamon and cumin
½ teaspoon each ground nutmeg, allspice and cayenne pepper

1 Combine salt and the boiling water in large non-metallic bowl; stir until salt dissolves. Stir in the cold water. Add onion, cauliflower, courgettes and celery; stand mixture overnight.

2 Rinse and drain vegetable mixture well; drain vegetables on absorbent paper.

3 Combine apple, garlic and 625ml of the vinegar in large saucepan; bring to the boil. Reduce heat; simmer, uncovered, about 10 minutes or until apple is soft. Remove from heat.

4 Blend cornflour with 35g of the vinegar in small jug until smooth. Add remaining vinegar, sugar and spices to pan; stir over high heat, without boiling, until sugar dissolves. Stir in cornflour mixture; cook, stirring, until mixture boils and thickens. Add vegetables; simmer, uncovered, about 5 minutes or until vegetables are tender.

5 Spoon hot pickle into hot sterilised jars; seal immediately. Label and date jars when cold.

prep + cook time 1 hour + standing time
makes 2.5 litres
nutritional count per tablespoon
0g total fat (0g saturated fat); 113kJ (27 cal); 6.5g carbohydrate; 0.3g protein; 0.4g fibre
tips Granny Smith apples are best for this recipe. Store pickle in a cool, dark place for at least three weeks before opening. Refrigerate after opening.

PICCALILLI

400g small pickling onions, peeled
140g coarse cooking salt
500ml boiling water
1.75 litres cold water
1 small cauliflower (1kg), cut into small florets
250g green beans, trimmed, chopped coarsely
2 medium carrots (240g), chopped coarsely
220g granulated sugar
50g plain flour
2 tablespoons mustard powder
2 teaspoons ground turmeric
½ teaspoon cayenne pepper
1 litre cider vinegar

1 Peel onions, leaving a tiny part of the roots intact to hold the onions together. Combine salt and the boiling water in large non-metallic heatproof bowl; stir until salt dissolves. Add the cold water. Add vegetables; mix well. Cover with a large plate or a sealed plastic bag half-filled with water to keep vegetables submerged; stand overnight.

2 Rinse and drain vegetables well; drain on absorbent paper.

3 Combine sugar, flour and spices in large saucepan; gradually whisk in vinegar until smooth. Cook, stirring, until mixture boils and thickens. Add vegetables; simmer, uncovered, about 10 minutes or until vegetables are barely tender.

4 Spoon hot piccalilli into hot sterilised jars; seal immediately. Label and date jars when cold.

prep + cook time 30 minutes + standing time
makes 2.5 litres
nutritional count per tablespoon 0g total fat (0g saturated fat); 59kJ (14 cal); 2.6g carbohydrate; 0.3g protein; 0.3g fibre
tip Store piccalilli in a cool, dark place for at least three weeks before opening. Refrigerate after opening.

BREAD & BUTTER PICKLE

500g unpeeled cucumbers,
  sliced thinly lengthways
1 large brown onion (200g),
  sliced thinly
70g coarse cooking salt
250ml white vinegar
220g granulated sugar
2 teaspoons mustard seeds
½ teaspoon dried chilli flakes
¼ teaspoon ground turmeric

1 Combine cucumber and onion in medium non-metallic bowl; sprinkle with salt, mix well. Cover; stand overnight.
2 Rinse and drain cucumber mixture; drain on absorbent paper. Spoon into hot sterilised jars.
3 Meanwhile, stir remaining ingredients in medium saucepan over high heat, without boiling, until sugar dissolves. Bring to the boil; remove from heat. Pour enough vinegar mixture into jars to cover cucumber mixture; seal immediately. Label and date jars when cold.

prep + cook time 30 minutes + standing time
makes 1 litre
nutritional count per tablespoon
0g total fat (0g saturated fat); 88kJ (21 cal); 5g carbohydrate; 0.1g protein; 0.2g fibre
tips Store pickle in a cool, dark place for at least three weeks before opening. Refrigerate after opening. The cucumbers will lose their colour on standing.

PICKLED ONIONS

1kg small pickling onions
140g coarse cooking salt
250ml boiling water
250ml cold water
2 fresh long red chillies, halved
 lengthways
750ml white wine vinegar
250ml white vinegar
165g unrefined granulated sugar
2 dried bay leaves
1 tablespoon black peppercorns

1 Place onions in large heatproof non-metallic bowl, cover with boiling water; stand 5 minutes, drain. Peel onions, leaving a tiny part of the roots intact to hold the onions together; return to bowl.

2 Combine salt and the boiling water in large heatproof jug; stir until salt dissolves. Add the cold water; pour over onions. Cover with a large plate or a sealed plastic bag half-filled with water to keep onions submerged; stand overnight.

3 Rinse and drain onions; pat onions dry with absorbent paper. Pack onions and chilli into hot sterilised jars.

4 Stir remaining ingredients in medium saucepan over high heat, without boiling, until sugar dissolves. Bring to the boil; remove from heat. Pour enough vinegar mixture into jars to cover onions; seal immediately. Label and date jars when cold.

prep + cook time 45 minutes + standing time
makes 1.5 litres
nutritional count per 60ml 0g total fat (0g saturated fat); 192kJ (46 cal); 9.1g carbohydrate; 0.6g protein; 0.6g fibre
tips Store pickle in a cool, dark place for at least three weeks before opening. Refrigerate after opening.

GARLIC CONFIT

7 medium garlic bulbs (500g),
    cloves separated, unpeeled
1 dried bay leaf
500ml olive oil, approximately

1 Preheat oven to 150°C/130°C fan-assisted.
2 Place garlic and bay leaf in small baking dish; add enough oil to dish to cover garlic. Roast, uncovered, about 45 minutes or until garlic is soft.
3 Spoon garlic and bay leaf into sterilised jars. Carefully pour enough of the oil left in dish into jars to cover garlic; seal immediately. Label and date jars when cold.

prep + cook time 50 minutes
makes 1 litre
nutritional count per tablespoon
0.5g total fat (0.1g saturated fat); 46kJ (11 cal); 0.6g carbohydrate; 0.4g protein; 1g fibre
tips To use, squeeze garlic flesh from the skins and stir through mayonnaise to make aïoli, or use in sauces and dips. Use a little of the garlic-infused olive oil as a tasty salad dressing. Store garlic confit in the refrigerator. Once opened, make sure garlic is always completely covered with oil; top up with a little more oil as necessary.

ONION JAM

60ml olive oil
1kg brown onions, sliced thinly
1 sprig fresh rosemary
160ml balsamic vinegar
110g light brown sugar

1 Heat oil in large saucepan; cook onion and rosemary, stirring occasionally, about 25 minutes or until onion is soft and browned lightly. Add vinegar; cook, stirring, about 5 minutes or until liquid is absorbed. Add sugar; cook, stirring, about 10 minutes or until onion is caramelised and jam is thick.
2 Spoon hot jam into hot sterilised jars; seal immediately. Label and date jars when cold.

prep + cook time 1 hour
makes about 560ml
nutritional count per tablespoon
4.6g total fat (0.6g saturated fat); 426kJ (102 cal); 13.4g carbohydrate; 1.2g protein; 1.1g fibre
tips Store onion jam in the refrigerator. Use a mandoline or V-slicer to slice onions as thinly as possible – it's much faster and easier than using a knife.

DRIED FRUIT RELISH

300g coarsely chopped dried
   apricots
280g coarsely chopped dried
   dates
375g dried figs, stems removed,
   chopped finely
750ml boiling water
330g light brown sugar
310ml cider vinegar
2 teaspoons coarse cooking salt

1 Combine fruit and the water in large saucepan; stand 30 minutes.
2 Add remaining ingredients to pan; stir over high heat, without boiling, until sugar dissolves. Bring to the boil. Reduce heat; simmer, uncovered, stirring occasionally, about 40 minutes or until relish is thick.
3 Spoon hot relish into hot sterilised jars; seal immediately. Label and date jars when cold.

prep + cook time 1 hour
+ standing time
makes 1.5 litres
nutritional count per tablespoon
0.1g total fat (0g saturated fat);
213kJ (51 cal); 11.7g carbohydrate;
0.5g protein; 1.5g fibre
tip Store relish in a cool, dark place for at least one week before opening. Refrigerate after opening.

CARAMELISED ONION & BEETROOT RELISH

2 tablespoons olive oil
4 large brown onions (800g),
 sliced thinly
330g light brown sugar
375ml cider vinegar
3 large fresh beetroot (600g),
 peeled, grated coarsely
1 teaspoon coarse cooking salt
½ teaspoon coarsely ground
 black pepper

1 Heat oil in large saucepan; cook onion, stirring, about 15 minutes or until onion is softened and caramelised.
2 Add remaining ingredients; stir over high heat, without boiling, until sugar dissolves. Bring to the boil. Reduce heat; simmer, uncovered, stirring occasionally, about 30 minutes or until beetroot is tender and relish is thick.
3 Spoon hot relish into hot sterilised jars; seal immediately. Label and date jars when cold.

prep + cook time 1 hour
makes 1 litre
nutritional count per tablespoon
0.8 g total fat (0.1g saturated fat); 184kJ (44 cal); 8.5g carbohydrate; 0.5g protein; 0.6g fibre
tips Wear disposable gloves when peeling beetroot as it will stain your hands. Store relish in a cool, dark place for at least three weeks before opening. Refrigerate the relish after opening.

INDIAN AUBERGINE RELISH

3 medium aubergines (900g)
2 teaspoons coarse cooking salt
2 tablespoons vegetable oil
½ teaspoon yellow mustard seeds
1 large red onion (300g), chopped finely
3 cloves garlic, crushed
2 fresh long green chillies, chopped finely
½ teaspoon cumin seeds
1 large tomato (220g), peeled, chopped finely
4 tablespoons fresh coriander leaves
3 tablespoons fresh mint leaves
1 teaspoon chilli powder
½ teaspoon ground turmeric
½ teaspoon tamarind paste
3 teaspoons coarse cooking salt, extra
250ml water

1 Peel alternate lengthwise strips of skin from aubergines; chop aubergines coarsely. Place aubergine in medium non-metallic bowl; sprinkle with salt, mix well. Stand 10 minutes. Rinse and drain aubergine well; drain on absorbent paper.

2 Heat oil in large frying pan; cook mustard seeds, stirring, until they begin to pop. Add onion, garlic, fresh chilli and cumin seeds; cook, stirring, until onion softens. Add tomato; cook, stirring, about 2 minutes or until tomato softens. Stir in aubergine and remaining ingredients; simmer, covered, over low heat, stirring occasionally, about 25 minutes or until aubergine is tender. Cool 15 minutes, then blend or process aubergine mixture until pulpy.

3 Spoon relish into hot sterilised jars; seal immediately. Label and date jars when cold.

prep + cook time 45 minutes + cooling time
makes 1.125 litres
nutritional count per tablespoon 0.7g total fat (0.1g saturated fat); 50kJ (12 cal); 0.9g carbohydrate; 0.3g protein; 0.6g fibre
tip The relish can be stored in the refrigerator for up to three weeks.

CORN RELISH

8 corn cobs (3.2kg), trimmed, kernels removed
2 medium red peppers (400g), chopped finely
1 large red onion (300g), chopped finely
2 stalks celery (300g), trimmed, chopped finely
220g granulated sugar
1 tablespoon yellow mustard seeds
3 teaspoons mustard powder
1 teaspoon ground turmeric
2 teaspoons coarse cooking salt
500ml cider vinegar
1½ tablespoons cornflour
2 tablespoons water

1 Stir vegetables, sugar, spices, salt and vinegar in large saucepan over high heat, without boiling, until sugar dissolves. Bring to the boil. Reduce heat; simmer, uncovered, stirring occasionally, for 25 minutes.
2 Blend cornflour with the water in small bowl until smooth; stir into vegetable mixture. Cook, stirring, until mixture boils and thickens. Pour into hot sterilised jars; seal immediately. Label and date jars when cold.

prep + cook time 1 hour
makes 2 litres
nutritional count per tablespoon 0.3g total fat (0g saturated fat); 155kJ (37 cal); 6.8g carbohydrate; 1.1g protein; 1.2g fibre
tip Relish will keep for several weeks in the refrigerator. Relish can be used straight away.

SAUCES &
CONDIMENTS

TOMATO SAUCE

2 tablespoons olive oil

2 medium brown onions (300g), chopped finely

3 cloves garlic, crushed

4cm piece fresh root ginger (20g), grated

1 teaspoon ground coriander

1kg ripe plum tomatoes, chopped coarsely

110g light brown sugar

80ml red wine vinegar

80ml white vinegar

1 teaspoon coarse cooking salt

1 Heat oil in large saucepan; cook onion, stirring, until softened. Add garlic, ginger and spice; cook, stirring, until fragrant. Stir in remaining ingredients. Bring to the boil. Reduce heat; simmer, uncovered, about 40 minutes or until tomatoes are soft and sauce thickens. Cool 15 minutes.

2 Blend or process mixture, in batches, until smooth; strain sauce through fine sieve into large heatproof bowl, discard solids. Return sauce to pan; bring to the boil, stirring.

3 Pour hot sauce into hot sterilised jars; seal immediately. Label and date jars when cold.

prep + cook time 50 minutes + cooling time

makes 750ml

nutritional count per tablespoon 1.1g total fat (0.1g saturated fat); 117kJ (28 cal); 4g carbohydrate; 0.4g protein; 0.5g fibre

variation For a spicy tomato sauce, add 1 finely chopped fresh long red chilli with the garlic in step 1.

BARBECUE SAUCE

2 tablespoons olive oil

2 medium brown onions (300g), chopped finely

5 cloves garlic, crushed

1kg ripe plum tomatoes, chopped coarsely

165g light brown sugar

125ml malt vinegar

80ml worcestershire sauce

1 teaspoon coarse cooking salt

1 Heat oil in large saucepan; cook onion, stirring, until softened. Add garlic; cook, stirring, until fragrant. Stir in remaining ingredients. Bring to the boil. Reduce heat; simmer, uncovered, about 1 hour or until tomatoes are soft and sauce is thickened. Cool 15 minutes.

2 Blend or process mixture, in batches, until smooth. Strain sauce through fine sieve into large heatproof bowl. Return sauce to pan; bring to the boil, stirring.

3 Pour hot sauce into hot sterilised jars; seal immediately. Label and date jars when cold.

prep + cook time 1 hour 30 minutes

makes about 560ml

nutritional count per tablespoon

1.4g total fat (0.2g saturated fat); 201kJ (48 cal); 7.9g carbohydrate; 0.6g protein; 0.7g fibre

tip It's much easier to check the consistency of the sauce after it has been blended and strained. If the sauce is too thin, return the sauce to the pan, bring it to the boil, then reduce the heat and simmer, uncovered, until reduced to about 560ml.

SWEET CHILLI SAUCE

200g fresh long red chillies,
  chopped coarsely
330g caster sugar
375ml white vinegar
4 cloves garlic, peeled
4cm piece fresh root ginger
  (20g), grated
½ teaspoon coarse cooking salt

1 Combine ingredients in medium saucepan; stir over high heat, without boiling, until sugar dissolves. Reduce heat; simmer, uncovered, about 45 minutes or until chilli is soft. Cool 10 minutes.
2 Blend or process mixture, in batches, until smooth.
3 Pour sauce into hot sterilised jars; seal immediately. Label and date jars when cold.

prep + cook time 1 hour
makes 435ml
nutritional count per tablespoon
0.1g total fat (0g saturated fat); 33kJ (8 cal); 16.2g carbohydrate; 0.2g protein; 1.1g fibre
tips Wear gloves when preparing the chillies as they can burn your skin. The hotness of the sauce will depend on the type of chillies used. Store in a cool, dark place for one week before opening. Sauce will keep in a cool, dark place for up to three months; refrigerate after opening. It will keep for several months in the refrigerator.

SMOKY TOMATO SAUCE

35g plain flour
40g loose tea leaves
1kg ripe plum tomatoes, halved
    lengthways
2 tablespoons olive oil
2 medium brown onions (300g),
    chopped finely
5 cloves garlic, crushed
110g light brown sugar
125ml white vinegar
1 teaspoon coarse cooking salt

1 Line large wok with foil; place flour and tea leaves in base of wok. Heat wok over medium-high heat until smoke appears. Place half the tomatoes, skin-side up, on small oiled wire rack inside wok. Cover wok; cook 10 minutes. Remove from heat; stand, covered, 10 minutes.
2 Heat oil in large saucepan; cook onion and garlic, stirring, until onion softens. Add all of the tomatoes and remaining ingredients; bring to the boil. Reduce heat; simmer, uncovered, stirring occasionally, about 40 minutes or until tomato softens and sauce is thick. Cool 15 minutes.
3 Blend or process tomato mixture, in batches, until smooth. Strain mixture through a fine sieve into large bowl; discard solids. Return to pan; bring to the boil.
4 Pour hot sauce into hot sterilised jars, seal immediately. Label and date jars when cold.

prep + cook time 1 hour 15 minutes + cooling time
makes 750ml
nutritional count per tablespoon
1.1g total fat (0.1g saturated fat); 117kJ (28 cal); 4g carbohydrate; 0.4g protein; 0.5g fibre
tips We used black tea leaves, but you could also use a smoky tea such as lapsang souchong. It's a good idea to do the smoking on the barbecue. Store sauce in the refrigerator.

TRADITIONAL ITALIAN TOMATO PASTA SAUCE

10kg very ripe plum tomatoes
2 good handfuls fresh basil leaves

1 Trim tops from tomatoes; cut tomatoes in half lengthways. Scrape out seeds.
2 Divide tomato halves into two large saucepans, or place in a large preserving pan; cook, covered, over low heat, stirring occasionally, about 30 minutes or until tomatoes begin to soften. Cool 10 minutes. Using a jug, carefully skim excess water from the surface of the tomatoes (about 375ml from each pan). Discard water.
3 Blend or process tomatoes, in batches, until smooth. Push purée through a fine sieve, in batches, into large bowl or jug; discard solids.
4 Pour tomato purée into hot sterilised bottles or jars (do not completely fill bottles or jars to the top – leave at least 2cm of space); push three basil leaves into each bottle. Seal immediately.
5 Wrap bottles in tea towels or several layers of newspaper; pack upright bottles tightly into large tall saucepan or preserving pan. Cover bottles with boiling water; bring to the boil. Boil for 1 hour, covered, replenishing water, as necessary, to maintain level. Cool bottles in water. Label and date bottles.

prep + cook time 3 hours + cooling time
makes 5.5 litres
nutritional count per 125ml 0.1g total fat (0g saturated fat); 63kJ (15 cal); 1.7g carbohydrate; 0.9g protein; 1.1g fibre
tips Store in a cool, dark place for up to 12 months; refrigerate after opening. If you have one, push the cooked tomato mixture through a mouli or food mill to remove the tomato skins, instead of following instructions for step 3; there is no need to blend the mixture first if pushing it through a mouli. Continue recipe from step 4. It is best to use either 500ml jars (serves 4) or 750ml jars (serves 6).

QUINCE PASTE

6 medium quinces (2.1kg)
375ml water
880g caster sugar

1 Peel, quarter and core quinces; tie cores in muslin. Coarsely chop quince flesh.
2 Combine quince flesh and muslin bag with the water in large saucepan; bring to the boil. Boil, covered, about 35 minutes or until fruit is soft; discard muslin bag.
3 Strain fruit over large heatproof bowl, reserving 125ml of the liquid; cool 10 minutes. Blend or process fruit with the reserved cooking liquid until smooth.
4 Return fruit mixture to pan with sugar; cook, stirring, over low heat, until sugar dissolves. Cook, over low heat, about 3½ hours, stirring frequently, until quince paste is very thick and deep ruby coloured.
5 Meanwhile, preheat oven to 100°C/90°C fan-assisted. Grease a loaf tin; line base with baking parchment, extending paper 5cm over long sides.
6 Spread paste into tin. Bake about 1½ hours or until surface is dry to touch. Cool paste in tin. Remove from tin; wrap in baking parchment, then in foil. Store in an airtight container in the refrigerator.

prep + cook time 6 hours + cooling time
makes 1.25 litres
nutritional count per tablespoon 0g total fat (0g saturated fat); 59kJ (14 cal); 17.3g carbohydrate; 0.1g protein; 1.3g fibre
tips When the paste is sufficiently cooked, a wooden spoon drawn through the paste will leave a very distinct trail across the base of the tin. To dry out the paste, you can also place it in a fan-assisted oven with only the fan working (no temperature set) overnight.

OVEN-DRIED TOMATOES

1kg ripe plum tomatoes, halved
   lengthways
2 teaspoons coarse cooking salt
½ teaspoon dried oregano
375ml olive oil

1 Preheat oven to 80°C/60°C fan-assisted.
2 Using a small sharp knife, score cut-sides of tomatoes lengthways, without cutting through the skin; push flesh outwards. Combine tomatoes, salt and oregano in large bowl; toss gently. Stand 10 minutes.
3 Place tomatoes, in a single layer, cut-side down, on an oiled wire rack, over large oven tray. Roast, uncovered, about 15 hours or until tomatoes are dry to touch.
4 Cool tomatoes on wire rack; pack into sterilised jars. Pour enough oil into jars to cover tomatoes; seal immediately. Label and date jars.

prep + cook time 15 hours 30 minutes + cooling time
makes about 26 pieces
nutritional count per piece 0.8g total fat (0.1g saturated fat); 54kJ (13 cal); 0.7g carbohydrate; 0.4g protein; 0.5g fibre
tips Tomatoes will keep, refrigerated, for up to 2 weeks; or freeze them in single layers, between sheets of baking parchment, in an airtight container for up to three months. Plum tomatoes are perfect for this recipe as they don't have many seeds; choose ripe unblemished tomatoes.

PRESERVED LEMONS

8 medium lemons (1.1kg)
450g rock salt
5 fresh bay leaves
1 teaspoon coriander seeds
1 teaspoon caraway seeds
250ml lemon juice

1 Halve lemons lengthways; carefully cut each lemon half in half again, without cutting all the way through. Open lemon halves out slightly.

2 Squeeze lemons over a large non-metallic bowl to catch the juice; add lemons to bowl with salt, bay leaves and seeds, mix well.

3 Pack lemon mixture into 1.5-litre sterilised jar; pour enough of the juice into the jar to cover lemons. Place a sealed small plastic bag filled with water on top of the lemons to keep them submerged; seal jar. Label and date jar.

prep + cook time 20 minutes
makes 16 pieces
nutritional count per piece
0.1g total fat (0.1g saturated fat); 88kJ (21 cal); 1.8g carbohydrate; 0.4g protein; 1.6g fibre

tips Store preserved lemons in a cool, dark place for at least three weeks before using. Refrigerate after opening. To use, remove and discard pulp, squeeze juice from rind, rinse rind well, then slice according to the recipe. Cinnamon sticks or chillies can be added to the preserved lemons in step 2.

CRACKED OLIVES

5kg green olives
2 tablespoons coarse cooking salt
2 cloves garlic, crushed
1 teaspoon dried chilli flakes
2 teaspoons dried mixed herbs
4 litres olive oil, approximately

1 Using a small hammer, or the flat side of a meat mallet, carefully crack each olive on a kitchen board, but do not remove stones. Place olives in large non-metallic bowl, plastic tub or bucket; cover with cold water. Cover with a large plate or a sealed plastic bag filled with water to keep olives submerged. Stand 12 to 16 days, changing the water every day, until olives become dark and tender. Drain.
2 Combine drained olives, salt, garlic, chilli and herbs in large strainer; stand in sink overnight. (Do not rinse olives.)
3 Spoon olives into sterilised jars; pour in enough olive oil to cover olives. Label and date jars.

prep + cook time 1½ hours + standing time
makes about 3kg drained olives
nutritional count per 60ml 2.2g total fat (0.3g saturated fat); 88kJ (21 cal); 0.4g carbohydrate; 0.2g protein; 0.4g fibre
tips You must use fresh, raw green olives, not those from the deli, as these have already been brined. These are available from specialist greengrocers and the internet. Store in a cool, dark place for at least two weeks before opening. Olives will keep for up to 12 months; refrigerate after opening. The amount of olive oil you will need depends on the size and shape of the jars used. Pack olives tightly into the jar but be gentle to avoid bruising. Olives may float to the surface; to keep them submerged, place a slice of lemon or a sealed small plastic bag filled with water on top of the olives before closing the jars. Warn anyone eating these olives that they still contain the stone.

CORDIALS & LIQUEURS

POMEGRANATE & RHUBARB CORDIAL

600g trimmed rhubarb, chopped
  coarsely
80ml water
625ml pomegranate pulp
220g caster sugar
1 teaspoon citric acid

1 Combine rhubarb and the water in medium saucepan; bring to the boil. Reduce heat; simmer, covered, about 10 minutes or until mixture is pulpy. Pour mixture through muslin-lined sieve into medium bowl. Stand 20 minutes, then squeeze muslin to extract more juice.

2 Meanwhile, place pomegranate in muslin-lined sieve over small bowl; squeeze muslin to extract as much juice as possible (you will need 250ml juice). Discard seeds (or save for another use).

3 Combine fruit juices, sugar and citric acid in medium saucepan; stir over high heat, without boiling, until sugar dissolves. Bring to the boil.

4 Pour hot syrup into hot sterilised bottles; seal immediately. Label and date bottles when cold. To serve, dilute the cordial with an equal amount of iced water or chilled sparkling mineral water, or serve undiluted, as a sauce, over ice-cream.

prep + cook time 35 minutes + standing time
makes 625ml
nutritional count per tablespoon (undiluted) 0.1g total fat (0g saturated fat); 46kJ (11 cal); 8.8g carbohydrate; 0.4g protein; 1g fibre
tips You will need about 1 bunch of rhubarb (use only the reddest stems) and 3 large pomegranates for this recipe. Store in the refrigerator for up to two weeks or freeze cordial in plastic bottles for up to three months; make sure you leave at least 2cm of space in the bottles to allow for expansion of liquid as it freezes.

PEACH & RASPBERRY CORDIAL

500g fresh raspberries
180ml water
1.5kg peaches, chopped coarsely, stones removed
1kg granulated sugar
1 teaspoon citric acid

1 Combine raspberries and 60ml of the water in medium saucepan; bring to the boil. Reduce heat; simmer, mashing with a potato masher, about 2 minutes or until pulpy. Pour mixture through muslin-lined sieve into medium bowl. Stand 20 minutes, then squeeze muslin to extract more juice.

2 Meanwhile, combine peaches and the remaining water in medium saucepan; simmer, covered, about 5 minutes or until mixture is pulpy. Mash peach mixture with a potato masher. Pour mixture through muslin-lined sieve into large bowl. Stand 20 minutes, then squeeze muslin to extract more juice.

3 Combine fruit juices, sugar and citric acid in medium saucepan; stir over high heat, without boiling, until sugar dissolves. Bring to the boil.

4 Pour hot syrup into hot sterilised bottles; seal immediately. Label and date bottles when cold. To serve, dilute the cordial with an equal amount of iced water or chilled sparkling mineral water, or serve undiluted, as a sauce, over ice-cream.

prep + cook time 35 minutes + standing time
makes 2 litres
nutritional count per tablespoon (undiluted) 0g total fat (0g saturated fat); 196kJ (47 cal); 11.6g carbohydrate; 0.2g protein; 0.5g fibre
tip Store in the refrigerator for up to two weeks.

LIMONCELLO

8 medium lemons (1.1kg)
750ml vodka
220g caster sugar
500ml water

1 Using a vegetable peeler, peel lemons thinly; discard any white pith from rind. Combine rind and vodka in 1-litre sterilised jar; seal. Stand jar in a cool, dark place for six days, shaking jar once a day.
2 To make sugar syrup, combine sugar and the water in medium saucepan; stir over high heat, without boiling, until sugar dissolves. Bring to the boil; remove from heat, cool.
3 Strain vodka through fine sieve into large bowl or jug; discard rind. Stir sugar syrup into vodka.
4 Pour limoncello into sterilised bottles; seal immediately. Label and date bottle. Refrigerate until cold before serving.

prep + cook time 30 minutes + standing & cooling time
makes 1.25 litres
nutritional count per tablespoon 0g total fat (0g saturated fat); 180kJ (43 cal); 4g carbohydrate; 0.1g protein; 0.4g fibre
tip Store limoncello in the refrigerator. We use the peel only from the lemons for this recipe. Once peeled, the lemons need to be refrigerated and used quickly.

PASSIONFRUIT & RUM LIQUEUR

220g caster sugar
500ml water
750ml white rum
250ml passionfruit pulp

1 Stir sugar and the water in medium saucepan over high heat, without boiling, until sugar dissolves; bring to the boil. Remove from heat; cool.
2 Stir in rum and passionfruit pulp. Pour liqueur into sterilised bottles; seal immediately. Label and date bottles.

prep + cook time 15 minutes + cooling
makes 1.25 litres
nutritional count per tablespoon 0g total fat (0g saturated fat); 176kJ (42 cal); 3.9g carbohydrate; 0.1g protein; 0.6g fibre
tips Store liqueur in the refrigerator for at least one week before serving. You will need about 10 passionfruit to get enough pulp for this recipe. You can leave the passionfruit seeds in the liqueur, or strain them out – the choice is yours.

CHERRIES IN BRANDY

1kg fresh cherries, stalks on
1 cinnamon stick
330g caster sugar
500ml brandy, approximately

1 Wash and dry cherries well. Place cherries and cinnamon in 1.5 litre sterilised jar; add sugar and enough brandy to cover cherries.

2 Seal jar; invert jar several times to help dissolve the sugar. Label and date jar.

3 Serve the cherries as a dessert with vanilla ice-cream. Drink the flavoured brandy as you would a liqueur.

prep + cook time 10 minutes + standing time
makes 1.5 litres
nutritional count per 60ml 0.1g total fat (0g saturated fat); 468kJ (112 cal); 17.3g carbohydrate; 0.3g protein; 0.5g fibre

tips Store cherries in a cool, dark place for at least 2 months before opening. Invert the jar every few days to help dissolve the sugar. Refrigerate after opening. Choose unblemished cherries. Remove the stalks from the cherries if you like. Pack cherries tightly into jar but be gentle to avoid bruising. Cherries will float to the surface; to keep them submerged, place a sealed small plastic bag filled with water on top of the cherries before closing the jar.

GLOSSARY

allspice also called pimento or jamaican pepper, tastes like a combination of nutmeg, cumin, clove and cinnamon – all spices. Available in ground form, or as whole berries.

bay leaves aromatic leaves from the bay tree available fresh or dried; used to add a strong, slightly peppery flavour to soups, stocks and casseroles.

caraway seeds a member of the parsley family; available in seed or ground form.

cardamom can be bought in pod, seed or ground form. Has a distinctive, aromatic, sweetly rich flavour.

cayenne pepper thin-fleshed, long, very-hot red chilli; usually purchased dried and ground.

chillies available in many types and sizes, both fresh and dried. The smaller the chilli, the hotter it is. Wear rubber gloves when handling chillies, as they can burn your skin. Removing seeds and membranes lessens the heat level.
flakes deep-red in colour; dehydrated, extremely fine slices and whole seeds; good for cooking or for sprinkling over cooked food.
green any unripened chilli; also some particular varieties that are ripe when green, such as jalapeño, habanero, poblano or serrano.
red available both fresh and dried; a generic term used for any moderately hot, long (about 6cm to 8cm), thin, chilli.
thai small, medium hot, and bright-red to dark-green in colour.

cinnamon dried inner bark of the shoots of the cinnamon tree. Available as a stick or ground.

citric acid commonly found in most fruits, especially limes and lemons. Commercial citric acid helps accentuate the acid flavour of fruit; it does not act as a preservative.

cloves can be used whole or in ground form. Has a strong scent and taste so should be used minimally.

coriander
leaves also known as cilantro or chinese parsley; bright-green leafy herb with a pungent flavour.
seeds the dried seeds of the coriander plant; coriander seeds and ground coriander must never be used to replace fresh coriander or vice versa. The tastes are completely different.

cornflour also known as cornstarch; used as a thickening agent in cooking.

cumin available both ground and as whole seeds; cumin has a warm, earthy, rather strong flavour.

fenugreek the leaves and seeds are available dried or ground; the seeds have a bitter taste. Often used in curries.

fish sauce also called nam pla or nuoc nam; made from pulverised salted fermented fish, mostly anchovies. Has a pungent smell and strong taste; use sparingly.

ginger
ground powdered ginger; cannot be substituted for fresh ginger.
root also called green or root ginger; the thick gnarled root of a tropical plant. Can be kept, peeled, covered with dry sherry in a jar and refrigerated, or frozen in an airtight container.

mustard
powder finely ground white (yellow) mustard seeds.

seeds yellow mustard seeds, also known as white mustard seeds, are ground and used for mustard powder and in most prepared mustards. Brown are also known as black mustard seeds; they are more pungent than the yellow variety and are used in curries. Available from major supermarkets and health-food shops.

nutmeg dried nut of an evergreen tree; available in ground form or you can grate your own with a fine grater.

onions

brown interchangeable with white onions; their pungent flesh adds flavour to a vast range of dishes.

red also known as Spanish, red Spanish or Bermuda onion; a sweet-flavoured, large, purple-red onion.

pickling small variety of onion especially suitable for pickling.

oregano also known as wild marjoram; has a woody stalk with clumps of tiny, dark green leaves that have a pungent, peppery flavour and are used fresh or dried.

salt

coarse cooking is coarser than table salt, but not as large-flaked as sea salt: it is sold in most supermarkets.

rock sold in large crystals, rock salt has a greyish hue because it is unrefined.

star anise a dried star-shaped pod, the seeds of which taste of aniseed.

sugar

caster also known as superfine; a finely granulated table sugar.

dark brown an extremely soft, fine-grained sugar retaining the deep flavour and colour of molasses.

light brown another soft, fine-grained sugar with cane molasses added.

granulated also known as crystal sugar, a coarse grain white table sugar.

unrefined natural brown granulated sugar.

tamarind paste a paste made from the hairy brown pods of the tamarind tree, each of which is filled with seeds and a viscous pulp which are are dried and

pressed into blocks. Releases a sweet-sour, slightly astringent taste.

treacle thick, dark syrup not unlike molasses; a by-product of sugar refining.

turmeric a member of the ginger family, its root is dried and ground; intensely pungent in taste but not hot.

vanilla pod dried long, thin pod from a tropical golden orchid grown in central and South America and Tahiti; the minuscule black seeds inside the bean are used to impart a distinctively sweet vanilla flavour.

vinegar

balsamic authentic only from the province of Modena, Italy; made from a regional wine of white trebbiano grapes specially processed then aged in antique wooden casks to give the exquisite pungent flavour.

malt made from fermented malt and beech shavings.

white made from spirit of cane sugar.

white wine/red wine based on fermented white/red wine.

INDEX

CONVERSION CHARTS

measures

One metric tablespoon holds 20ml; one metric teaspoon holds 5ml.

All cup and spoon measurements are level. The most accurate way of measuring dry ingredients is to weigh them. When measuring liquids, use a clear glass or plastic jug with metric markings.

We use large eggs with an average weight of 60g.

dry measures

METRIC	IMPERIAL
15g	½oz
30g	1oz
60g	2oz
90g	3oz
125g	4oz (¼lb)
155g	5oz
185g	6oz
220g	7oz
250g	8oz (½lb)
280g	9oz
315g	10oz
345g	11oz
375g	12oz (¾lb)
410g	13oz
440g	14oz
470g	15oz
500g	16oz (1lb)
750g	24oz (1½lb)
1kg	32oz (2lb)

liquid measures

METRIC	IMPERIAL
30ml	1 fluid oz
60ml	2 fluid oz
100ml	3 fluid oz
125ml	4 fluid oz
150ml	5 fluid oz
190ml	6 fluid oz
250ml	8 fluid oz
300ml	10 fluid oz
500ml	16 fluid oz
600ml	20 fluid oz
1000ml (1 litre)	32 fluid oz

length measures

3mm	⅛in
6mm	¼in
1cm	½in
2cm	¾in
2.5cm	1in
5cm	2in
6cm	2½in
8cm	3in
10cm	4in
13cm	5in
15cm	6in
18cm	7in
20cm	8in
23cm	9in
25cm	10in
28cm	11in
30cm	12in (1ft)

oven temperatures

These are fan-assisted temperatures. If you have a conventional oven (ie. not fan-assisted), increase temperatures by 10–20°.

	°C (CELSIUS)	°F (FAHRENHEIT)	GAS MARK
Very low	100	210	½
Low	130	260	1–2
Moderately low	140	280	3
Moderate	160	325	4–5
Moderately hot	180	350	6
Hot	200	400	7–8
Very hot	220	425	9